Sam, Sam, Sam

by Linda Cave
illustrated by Meryl Henderson

Core Decodable 6

McGraw Hill Education

Bothell, WA • Chicago, IL • Columbus, OH • New York, NY

MHEonline.com

Send all inquiries to:
McGraw-Hill Education
8787 Orion Place
Columbus, OH 43240

ISBN: 978-0-02-145326-9
MHID: 0-02-145326-8

Printed in Canada.

9 10 11 12 KOD 24

I am Sam.

I am Sam.

I am Sam.

Sam?

Sam, Sam, Sam.

I am Sam.